GW01236998

It's Official: Print from World

Selected by Sue Wright and David Orme

Contents

Longman

Edinburgh Gate
Harlow, Essex

The entire population was involved in the war in one way or another. Even children had to 'do their bit' in wartime when adults were working long hours doing war work 'on the home front'.

Simple Jobs That Boys Can Do Themselves – and So Help Win The War

How to PATCH LINO

A worn or frayed place in the lino can be neatly repaired providing you have an extra bit to match. First cut out the worn part with a sharp knife. Place this piece on the new piece – taking pains to match the design if there is one – and, using it as a guide, cut out a new piece exactly the same size. Glue the back of the new piece very carefully and place it in the hole, pressing it down well. It should scarcely show at all.

How to clear a CHOKED SINK

Place a pail under the screw cap at the bottom of the U-bend or trap and undo this cap with the aid of a strong bar – a screwdriver shaft, say. A rush of water will come directly the cap is off and it will bring accumulations of hair, etc., with it. But if the pipe is still stopped up, poke it clear with a stick inserted at the sink end. Be sure to screw the cap on again securely.

Sometimes a sink can be cleared if the stoppage is not too stubborn by placing the palm of the hand or a swabbing cloth over the opening and rapidly lifting it up and down, causing suction.

Useful Jobs That Girls Can Do – To Help Win The War

Girls simply must be able to use their needles neatly in wartime – here are a few hints on sewing for beginners. But needlework isn't enough, in these days when EVERYTHING must be made the most of; see if you can't turn your hand to other jobs around the house

Don't buy NEW for a CUSHION COVER

If a cushion needs a new cover, make one in patchwork, using odd bits from the scrap bag. Silk or velvet scraps would be lovely and soft – but odds and ends of dress woollens will last longer. Trim your pieces to the shapes you want and tack them to a square of news-paper cut to the right size. Then machine or feather stitch them together, taking care to get the joins smooth and flat. Use the best side of the existing cover to back the cushion.

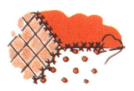

The Channel Islands was the only British territory invaded by the Germans. The islands were occupied from 1940 until 1945. During that time, any resistance was dealt with very severely, as this poster from 1941 shows.

NOTICE:

LOUIS BERRIER,

a resident of Ernes is charged with having released a pigeon with a message for England. He was, therefore, sentenced

TO DEATH

for espionage by the Court Martial and

SHOT

on the 2nd of August.

August 3rd, 1941.   Court Martial.

In the early days of the war there was a serious danger of invasion. This leaflet told civilians what to do if the enemy arrived.

Issued by the Ministry of Information on behalf of the War Office and the Ministry of Home Security

STAY WHERE YOU ARE

If this island is invaded by sea or air everyone who is not under orders must stay where he or she is. This is not simply advice; it is an order from the government, and you must obey it just as soldiers obey their orders. Your order is "Stay Put", **but remember this does not apply until the invasion comes**.

Why must I stay put?

Because in France, Holland and Belgium, the Germans were helped by the people who took flight before them. Great crowds of refugees blocked all roads. The soldiers who could have defended them could not get at the enemy. The enemy used the refugees as a human shield. These refugees were got out on to the roads by rumour and false orders. Do not be caught out in this way. Do not take any notice of any story telling about what the enemy has done or where he is. Do not take orders except from the Military, the Police, the Home Guard (L.D.V.) and the A.R.P. authorities or wardens.

What will happen to me if I don't stay put?

If you do not stay put you will stand a very good chance of being killed. The enemy may machine-gun you from the air in order to increase panic, or you may run into enemy forces which have landed behind you. An official German message was captured in Belgium which ran:

"Watch for civilian refugees on the roads. Harass them as much as possible."

Our soldiers will be hurrying to drive back the invader and will not be able to stop and help you. On the contrary, they will have to turn you off the roads so that they can get at the enemy. You will not have reached safety and you will have done just what the enemy wanted you to do.

How shall I prepare to stay put?

Make ready your air raid shelter; if you have no shelter prepare one. Advice can be obtained from your local Air Raid Warden or in "Your Home as an Air Raid Shelter", the Government booklet which tells you how to prepare a shelter in your house that will be strong enough to protect you against stray shots and falling metal. If you have a trench ready in your garden or field, so much the better, especially if you live where there is likely to be danger from shell-fire.

How can I help?

You can help by setting a good example to others. Civilians who try to join in the fight are more likely to get in the way than to help. The defeat of an enemy attack is the task of the armed forces which include the Home Guard, so if you wish to fight enrol in the Home Guard. If there is no vacancy for you at the moment register your name for enrolment and you will be called upon as soon as the Army is ready to employ you. For those who cannot join there are many ways in which the Military and Home Guard may need your help in their preparations. Find out what you can do to help in any local defence work that is going on, and be ready to turn your hand to anything if asked by the Military or Home Guard to do so.

If you are responsible for the safety of a factory or some other important building, get in touch with the nearest military authority. You will then be told how your defence should fit in with the military organisation and plans.

What shall I do if the Invader comes my way?

If fighting by organised forces is going on in your district and you have no special duties elsewhere, go to your shelter and stay there until the battle is past. Do not attempt to join in the fight. Behave as if an air raid were going on. The enemy will seldom turn aside to attack separate houses.

But if small parties are going about threatening persons and property in an area not under enemy control and come your way, you have the right of every man and woman to do what you can to protect yourself, your family and your home.

Stay put.

It's easy to say. When the time comes it may be hard to do. But you have got to do it; and in doing it you will be fighting Britain's battle as bravely as a soldier.

WAR EMERGENCY

INFORMATION AND INSTRUCTIONS

Read this leaflet carefully and make sure that you and all other responsible persons in your house understand its contents.

Pay no attention to rumours. Official news will be given in the papers and over the wireless.

Listen carefully to all broadcast instructions and be ready to note them down.

For the first time, not only soldiers but all civilians were involved in the war in what was known as the Home Front. The greatest danger was air raids. This leaflet from the Ministry of Information gave advice and instructions to householders.

(1) INFORMATION AND INSTRUCTIONS FOR THE PUBLIC.

Information and instructions will be given to the public by means of broadcast announcements. These announcements are of vital importance to everyone. Listen carefully and have a pencil and paper ready so that you may make a note of anything that concerns you, and inform other persons in your household who have not heard the broadcast. Announcements will be made in all News Bulletins and at special times which will be announced beforehand.

(2) IDENTITY LABELS.

You should carry about with you your full name and address clearly written. This should be on an envelope, card or luggage label, not on some odd piece of paper easily lost. In the case of children a label should be sewn on to their clothes, in such a way that it cannot easily come off.

(3) AIR RAID WARNINGS.

Warnings of air raids will be given in town and suburban areas by sirens or hooters. In some places the warning will be a series of short blasts and in other places a warbling or fluctuating signal which rises or falls every few seconds. The warning may also be given by police or air raid wardens blowing short blasts on whistles.

Directly you hear any of these sounds you should take cover if you can. Stay in your place of shelter until you hear the "Raiders Passed" signal which will be given by sounding the sirens or hooters continuously for a period of two minutes on the same note.

If poison gas has been used, you will be warned by means of hand rattles. If you hear hand rattles you must not leave your shelter until the poison gas has been cleared away. Hand bells will be used to tell you when there is no longer any danger from poison gas.

Make sure that everyone in your house understands the meanings of these signals.

(4) LIGHTING RESTRICTIONS.

All windows, skylights, glazed doors and other openings which would show a light at night must be screened with dark blinds, curtains, or blankets, or with brown paper fixed on to the glass so that no light is visible from the outside. All lighted signs and advertisement lights must be turned out.

All street lighting will be stopped till further notice.

(5) FIRE PRECAUTIONS AND METHOD OF DEALING WITH INCENDIARY BOMBS.

Clear the top floor of all inflammable materials, lumber, etc. See that you can get easily to any attic or roof spaces.

Water is the best means of putting out a fire started by an incendiary bomb. See that water is available about the house. Have some ready in buckets, but do not draw off water if you can help it during an air raid. Be careful not to throw a bucket of water directly over a burning incendiary bomb. The bomb would explode and throw burning fragments in all directions.

You may be able to smother a small bomb with sand or dry earth.

(6) CLOSING OF CINEMAS, THEATRES AND PLACES OF ENTERTAINMENT.

All cinemas, theatres, dance halls and places of public entertainment will be closed until further notice. When it is seen how the air attacks develop it may be possible to allow the re-opening of such places in some areas. They are being closed because if they were hit by a bomb, large numbers would be killed or injured. Football matches and outdoor meetings of all kinds which bring large numbers together are prohibited until further notice. Never crowd together unnecessarily.

GENERAL INSTRUCTIONS.

Carry your gas mask with you always.

Do not allow your children to run about the streets.

Avoid waste of any kind whether of food, water, electricity or gas.

Obey promptly any instructions given to you by the police, the special constables, the air raid wardens, or any other authorised persons and be ready to give them any assistance for which they ask you.

DO NOT TAKE TOO MUCH NOTICE OF NOISE IN AN AIR RAID. MUCH OF IT WILL BE THE NOISE OF OUR OWN GUNS DEALING WITH THE RAIDERS.

KEEP A GOOD HEART. WE ARE GOING TO WIN THROUGH.

Tell NOBODY—
not even HER

CARELESS TALK COSTS LIVES

A FEW
CARELESS WORDS
MAY END IN THIS—

Many lives were lost in the last war through careless talk
Be on your guard! Don't discuss movements of ships or troops

CARELESS TALK
COSTS LIVES

13

The government thought it likely that the enemy would drop poison gas onto the population from aircraft. Early in the war everyone – including babies – was given a gas mask, which had to be carried at all times. In the event, gas was not used and the gas masks were not needed.

YOUR GAS MASK

TAKE CARE OF YOUR GAS MASK AND YOUR GAS MASK WILL TAKE CARE OF YOU. It is possible that in war your life might depend on your gas mask and the condition in which it has been kept.

The official gas mask, or respirator, consists of a metal container filled with material which absorbs the gas, and a rubber face-piece with a non-inflammable transparent window. Some people seem to think that this mask does not look as if it would offer very good protection. Actually, it has been most carefully designed and fully tested, and will give you adequate protection against breathing any of the known war gases. But remember it will not protect you from the ordinary gas that you burn in a gas cooker or gas fire.

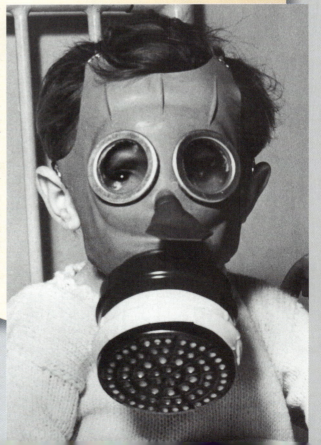

HOW TO STORE IT

Your mask should be kept carefully. Never hang it up by the straps which fasten it over the head. This will pull the rubber face-piece out of shape so that it no longer fits you properly. It should be kept in the special box provided, where this has been issued, but any box which is air-tight, or nearly so, will do.

When placed in the box the metal container should lie flat with the rubber facepiece uppermost, the transparent window lying evenly on top at full length. Great care should be taken not to bend or fold the window, or to let it get scratched, cracked or dented.

Keep the box in a cool place away from strong light. Exposure to heat or prolonged exposure to strong light will spoil the material of the mask and it may cease to give complete protection. It should never be held close to a fire or hot water pipes, or left lying out in the sun.

HOW TO PUT IT ON AND TAKE IT OFF

It is important to know how to put on your mask quickly and properly. You might need to do this in a hurry. To put it on, hold the mask by each of the side straps with the thumbs underneath and the inside of the window facing you. Then lift the mask to your face, push your chin forwards into it and draw the straps over the top of your head as far as they will go. See that the straps are properly adjusted and leave them so.

To remove the mask, insert the thumb under the buckle at the back of your head and then pull it forward over the top of your head so that the mask is lowered downwards from the face.

NEVER TRY TO LIFT THE MASK OFF UPWARDS OR BY PULLING THE CONTAINER OR THE EDGE OF THE RUBBER AT THE CHIN.

To prevent the window from misting over when the mask is worn, wet the end of a finger and rub it on a piece of toilet soap. Then rub the finger all over the inside of the window as to leave a thin film of soap.

PUTTING YOUR MASK AWAY

After the mask has been used you will find that it is wet on the inside with moisture from the breath. This should be wiped off with a soft dry cloth and the mask allowed to dry before it is put away in its box. Do not try to dry it by applying heat.

The contents of the container do not deteriorate either with age or with wearing the mask when gas is not present. But if you suspect any flaw in your gas mask you should inform your local air raid warden.

It is a good thing to get out your gas mask occasionally and put it on, so as to get used to wearing it, and if you take the simple precautions set out above you will ensure that it is always ready for your protection.

Marylebone Borough Council produced a helpful poem so that people would know what to do if gas was dropped from aircraft. This is part of it.

Blister Gas

When you have heard the
    warning sound

That mustard gas is on
    the ground,

Put on the mask that you possess;

All helpers have protective dress.

Remember, 'tis persistent gas,

Will last for weeks on roads
    or grass.

The smallest splash upon
    your hand

Will quickly to a sore expand.

If on a person there's a trace,

Rush him to the appointed place.

Take off his boots and clothes
    and suit

And scrub him well from head
    to foot,

Then in another room he'll find

Fresh clothes and boots, assistance kind.

Choking Gases

Phosgene and Chlorine are, alas,

Chloropicrin too, a deadly gas.

Affects the lungs, affects
    the breath,

And very soon may lead to death.

The only hope is perfect rest:

Remember this and do your best.

Pop on a mask, and quickly
    fetch her

Without the least delay,
    a stretcher.

Don't let her move, give her
    beef tea,

Keep her as warm as she can be.

Don't give her alcoholic drinks;

Persuade her to have
    'forty winks'.

And in spite of great temptation

Don't try artificial respiration.

Marylebone Borough Council

It was soon realised that the major cities would suffer most from enemy bombing. It was decided that children should be evacuated to safer places in the country, and by early 1940 many children were sent out of the cities. Often a whole school would go together, along with their teachers.

Not every family wanted to send their children away, and some children returned to their families. In March of 1940 there were still many children in London. The Government asked the local authorities to organise a further evacuation. This is part of the leaflet that was sent out by the London County Council.

London County Council

19th March, 1940.

THE GOVERNMENT'S EVACUATION SCHEME
PLAN IV.

INTRODUCTION

An important circular recently issued to local authorities by the Ministry of Health sets out the present policy of the government in regard to evacuation. The policy may be summarised as follows:

(i) The dispersal of children from the evacuating areas is as desirable now as it was at the outbreak of war.

(ii) It is a vital part of the war effort to encourage the retention in the receiving areas of those children who are already there.

(iii) A plan is to be made for a further evacuation of school children, on the understanding that the plan will be carried into effect only if air raids develop "on a scale involving serious and continuing perils to civilian population".

(iv) Children evacuated under these arrangements will travel in organised parties under the charge of teachers from some or all of the evacuating areas of the country. The Government will decide when the plan for the metropolitan evacuating area shall be put into operation.

MOVING OFF

A squad of 30 children will be regarded as a unit for marching purposes. As far as possible, children of a family should be in the same squad. Younger children get more assistance from seniors if spread through the party, avoiding the rear, and in marching in fours they travel best on the inside.

Where parties have to cross busy roads in proceeding to the station it will be found that much time will be saved if the party adopts the 'wave' method of crossing. By this method the whole party halts in column formation on one side of the road, the traffic is held up at both ends of the column, and the party crosses the road in one wave, maintaining formation.

Parties to be conveyed by road from assembly point to entraining station must form two deep at the "picking up point". Both files will board the bus or tram together, the left-hand file going inside and the right-hand file on top. As far as possible the smaller children should travel inside.

If an air raid warning is given on the way to the entraining station, the directions of the police or air raid wardens must be followed; if after entrainment, the directions of the railway officials.

GAS MASKS

All adults and children should take their gas masks, which should be slung over the shoulder and not packed in luggage. The name and home address of the owner should be written on the webbing.

LUGGAGE CARRIERS

The most satisfactory luggage carrier is a rucksack, which leaves the arms free.

IDENTITY CARDS AND RATION BOOKS

All adults and children should have with them their Identity Cards and their Ration Books. These articles are to be packed in such a way, e.g. in a pocket of the rucksack, that they can be readily produced on arrival. If a child should arrive in the country without a Ration Book, the Leader of the party will notify the Local Food Office.

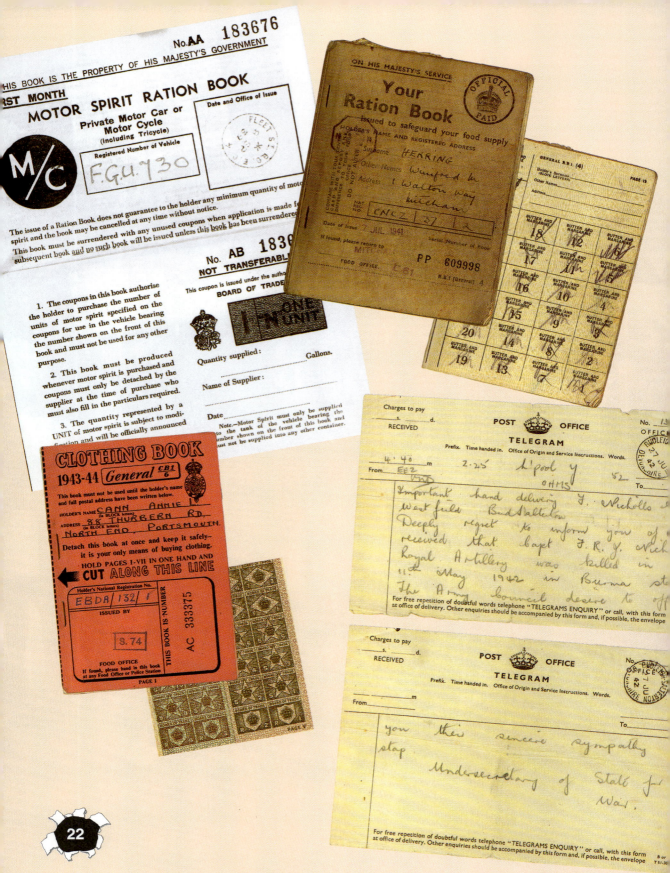

NISTRY OF AGRICULTURE AND FISHERIES
WOMEN'S LAND ARMY

Surrey _County Secretary_

Address Education Office, Park Street,
Guildford.

Telephone No. : Guildford 2053/4

Miss Lang,

NOTIFICATION OF TRAINING

A four weeks' training in hand and machine milking starting on
y, 11th May 1942 has been arranged for you, as a
er of the Women's Land Army, with Dauntsey School
West Lavington, Devizes

; training you will be billeted at Mrs. Andrews, Spin Hill, Market
Lavington, Devizes

arest station is Lavington

should arrive on Monday, 11th May 1942 Please notify
of the time of your arrival as soon as
e. **[P.T.O.**

6.—Sickness or Accident.—Directly you arrive at your place of training obtain a
ical Card from the nearest Post Office if you have not one already and arrange to
e your name entered on the Health Insurance Panel of a nearby doctor. **Do not**
; to do this until you are ill.

If you are unable to continue your training on account of illness or accident, call
our panel doctor and tell your County Secretary at once. You will not receive any
onal Allowance during your period of incapacity. If you are able to do so you
ld return home and you may then apply for a refund of your travelling expenses.

In the years when our Country
was in mortal danger

HERBERT JAMES HERMAN

who served 17th June, 1942 - 31st December, 1944

gave generously of his time and
powers to make himself ready
for her defence by force of arms
and with his life if need be.

George R.I.

THE HOME GUARD

NATIONAL REGISTRATION IDENTITY CARD

NATIONAL SERVICE (ARMED FORCES) ACT, 1939
ENLISTMENT NOTICE

**SHOULD TAKE
HIS NOTICE
H YOU WHEN
OU REPORT**

MINISTRY OF LABOUR AND NATIONAL SERVICE
EMPLOYMENT EXCHANGE,
Divisional Office,
281-9, Corporation Street,
Birmingham, 4.

Date 26th March, 1940.

Mr. H. J. Griffin,
55, New Road,
NETHERTON, NR. DUDLEY.

Registration No. DLR. 1908.

DEAR SIR,
In accordance with the National Service (Armed Forces) Act, 1939, you are called
upon for service in the Territorial Army, and are required to present yourself
on Tues day 2nd April, 19 40, at 10 a.m, or as early
as possible thereafter on that day, to :— between 9 a.m. and 12 noon

Royal Artillery, 59 Division Medium Regiment,

Drill Hall, Victoria Rd., Hanley, Staffs.

Stoke-on-Trent. (nearest railway station).

Delete
if not
applic- A Travelling Warrant for your journey is enclosed. Before starting your journey you
able must exchange the warrant for a ticket at the booking office named on the warrant. If
possible, this should be done a day or two before you are due to travel.
A Postal Order for 4s. in respect of advance of service pay, is also enclosed. Uniform
and personal kit will be issued to you after joining H.M. Forces. Any kit that you take with
you should not exceed an overcoat, change of clothes, stout pair of boots, and personal kit,
such as razor, hair brush, tooth brush, soap and towel.
Immediately on receipt of this notice, you should inform your employer of the date
upon which you are required to report for service.

Yours faithfully,
J. BEST.
for Divisional Controller. _Manager._

N.S. 12 (4884) Wt. 27900—6813 9/39 B.W. 677

Many families were kept busy early in the war building simple air raid shelters. These consisted of curved sheets of corrugated steel buried in a hole in the garden and covered over with earth. They could not protect people from a direct hit, but would shelter them from shrapnel and falling rubble.

The Anderson shelter, as it was called, was not very comfortable, particularly in winter. They often filled with water, and were usually cold and damp. The Ministry of Home Security issued a helpful leaflet showing ways in which people could improve conditions in their shelters.

WHEN YOU GO TO SHELTER

Your Anderson shelter this Winter

ISSUED BY THE MINISTRY OF HOME SECURITY

HOW YOU AND YOUR FAMILY CAN SLEEP IN COMFORT

WITH A LITTLE trouble and at very little cost you can make your Anderson steel shelter a comfortable winter sleeping place for your family.

Four adults and four babies, for example, or four adults and two older children can find sleeping room in a standard Anderson shelter 6 ft 6 in in length.

HOW TO MAKE BUNKS FOR YOUR SHELTER

A HAMMER, some nails and a saw, and possibly a pair of pliers that will cut wire are all the tools you will need. The materials are a few feet of timber, not less that $1\frac{7}{8}$ in square, some nails, and some canvas (or hessian, burlap, stout wire netting or similar material).

Look at the diagram of the arrangements of bunks and you will at once see the idea. The top bunks run from one end of the shelter to the other, the ends resting on angle-irons that run horizontally across the shelter at each end. These bunks should be 20 in wide, and about 6 ft 6 in long.

The lower bunks are the same size, but rest on the floor of the shelter, on feet or legs that will keep them at least 4 in off the floor.

The cross bunks for the children are 4 ft 6 in long, and have four legs, each 14 in high, which rest on the side-pieces of the lengthways bunks. The cross bunks can be up to 2 ft wide or even a little more.

Fix your canvas, hessian, wire netting, etc across the bunk frames, and the job is finished. Your local Council may be able to help you to obtain the timber.

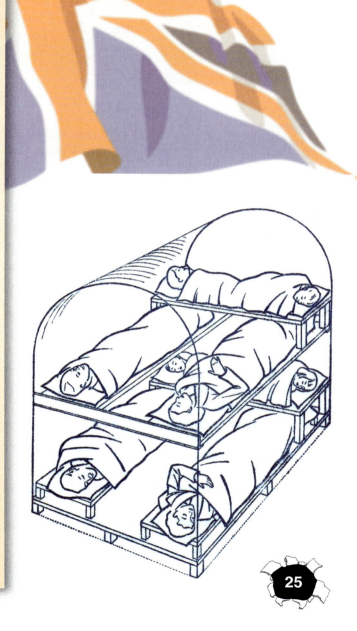

HEATING THE SHELTER

AN IMPROVISED HEATER can be made with two large flowerpots and a candle. Fix the candle in one of the flowerpots and place it on the ground with something underneath to raise the base just clear of the ground. Light the candle and invert the second flowerpot on top of the first. The candle will not burn enough oxygen to do any harm. As the upper flowerpot warms up it will give off a great deal of heat. A kettle of water can be placed on the top; it should have something underneath it to raise it just clear of the flowerpot.

WHEN YOU GO TO SHELTER

BEFORE YOU LEAVE the house, turn off all gas taps, including pilot jets, and turn the gas off at the main. Leave buckets or cans of water and sand or earth on the front door step, or just inside the door. Put your stirrup pump, if you have one, where it can be easily seen. Draw back all curtains and raise blinds in upper rooms so that any fires which may be started may be visible from the outside. This may save your house. Take with you your money and any valuables and documents, such as rent book, or building society book, insurance policy, records of instalment payments, etc.

WHAT TO TAKE WITH YOU

IDENTITY CARDS, ration books, etc. Gas masks. Hot drink. Shaded torch. Simple first-aid articles. Hot-water bottles or bricks. A bottle of water in case anyone is thirsty during the night.

A tin of biscuits in case the children wake up hungry in the night.

SOME GENERAL HINTS

IF, AS MAY FREQUENTLY HAPPEN, you spend the evening in your shelter before going to bed, you may want to read or knit, for example. Take care of your eyes. A good light can be obtained from candlelamps or a night light. Oil lamps are dangerous as they may get spilled either by shock from a bomb or by accident. There is not the same objection to the use of a lamp while you are awake as there is after you are asleep; if the air should become very foul, you would know it long before the danger point is reached, which might not be the case if you were asleep. But of course you must take care that no light is visible from the outside. If you have been using such a light, however, clear the air in the shelter before you settle down to sleep, otherwise you will have a disturbed night.

If you take your dog into your shelter, you should muzzle him. Dogs are liable to become hysterical if bombs explode nearby.

In case your house is destroyed you should try to make plans now to go and stay with friends or relations who live near you – but not too near. They should also arrange now to come to you if their house is knocked out.

Your own vegetables all the year round...

if you

DIG FOR VICTORY NOW

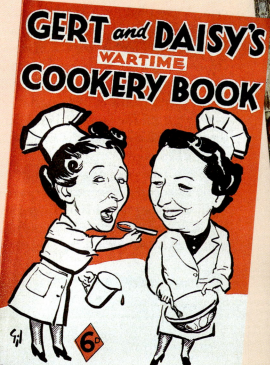

GERT and DAISY'S WARTIME COOKERY BOOK

6d

FOOD FACTS FOR THE KITCHEN FRONT

A Book of Wartime Recipes and Hints
WITH A FOREWORD BY
LORD WOOLTON
Price Sixpence

O

T

mean

really help us to win the w

people all contributing, be

Many people make tea by a

As a companion to this leaflet
the Ministry of Food
have issued a leaflet

6 STARS FROM the WINTER GARDEN

SAVOY THE BIG-HEARTED TENOR

SPINACH THE STRONGEST MAN IN THE WORLD

KALE THE EVER GREEN

THE LEEKS THEY KNOW THEIR ONIONS

IF IT'S HEALTH YOU'RE AFTER CABBAGE YOU LUCKY PEOPLE

THE SPROUT SISTERS Very tasty – very sweet

GROW THEM IN YOUR WIN...

OD · OUR DEFENCE

Defence runs through all our homes. It is where we must
guard. The watchword is careful housekeeping.

...ple, this urgent duty, that we may tend to overlook its full
...g here and there—how can that
...and there, with our 45 million
...e amount. Take one example.
...onful a head, and an additional
...e pot." The teaspoonful "for
...ssary. It is equal over the whole
...y shiploads a year. We must have those ships to bring

...ow much of our food comes from overseas—more than
...peace-time year.   Let us picture the convoys, bringing
...hores and let us be very careful.

The KITCHEN FRONT

122 WARTIME RECIPES
broadcast by Frederick Grisewood,
Mabel Constanduros and others, speci-
ally selected by the Ministry of Food.

6ᴰ NET

Rationing of food led to concerns that children in particular would suffer from an inadequate diet in view of the severe shortages. This information comes from a leaflet produced by the Ministry of Food.

Your Children's FOOD IN WARTIME

You want your children to be happy and healthy, of course; and to grow up strong and sturdy. Do you know that all depends upon the food you give them now, and the food habits you help them to form? By following the few simple rules given in this leaflet, you can do much to make sure that your children build sound constitutions and healthy, active bodies.

Foods That Build Bones, Muscle and Teeth

1 Milk

A Take advantage of the Government's milk schemes. See that your child gets all the "priority" milk he or she is entitled to at home, and that school children get milk in school wherever possible.

B See that each child in the family actually consumes his or her full allowance of milk, and that it is not given to any grown-up.

C Use the National Household Skimmed Milk as an extra when it is obtainable.

D Use milk in vegetable soups and stews, as well as in puddings, sauces and drinks.

2 Cheese

Ⓐ Give each child over two years of age the full ration.

Ⓑ From one year onward, toddlers can have dried grated cheese served with vegetables or as sandwiches.

Ⓒ Stretch the ration out over the week and serve with vegetables, wholemeal or wheatmeal bread or with pulses (beans, peas, lentils) for older children.

3 Eggs

Give each child under six years the full ration of eggs provided under the priority scheme. If using them in cooking, see that the children, and the children only, are served with the dishes made from their allowance of eggs. For those over six years, the best alternatives to eggs are:

Ⓐ Liver, when obtainable.

Ⓑ Sardines, salmon, pilchards, herrings or any other oily fish.

Ⓒ Increased quantities of pulses, green vegetables and wholemeal or wheatmeal bread.

4 Meat

Ⓐ Each child over two years should have his or her full ration of meat.

Ⓑ Do not give the man or other grown-up members of the household the children's meat. They are not growing and do not need it so much as the children, particularly the children at school or those under twenty-one years of age who are at work.

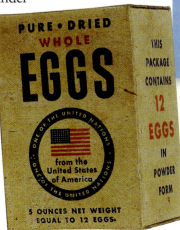

Ⓒ Do not serve the whole of the week's ration in two or three days. Stretch it out over the week, serving it with pulses, oatmeal, or wholemeal or wheatmeal bread or pastry.

5 Fish

Ⓐ Give the children their fair share of the fish bought on the points ration.

Ⓑ Use fresh salted cod or smoked cod at least once or twice a week. Make it into dishes with potato or vegetables. Do not serve it plain with sauce.